To My Beautiful Wife, Kelsey.

Without You, I'd Be the Only Sanchez-Trapp on Earth.

Contents

A Quick Bit About the Author — Pages I - III

Preface — Page V

Chapter 1 — Pages 1 & 2
Money, The Glue That Binds Us

Chapter 2 — Pages 3 - 16
The Basics Everyone Should Know

Chapter 3 — Pages 17 - 22
The "B" Word

Final Thoughts — Page 23

Sanchez-WHO???

Greetings to all my fellow Millennials and maybe a few Centennials and Gen-X's. I am glad you stumbled upon my little diamond in the rough.

My name is Joe Sanchez-Trapp and I'm going to take you through a little history about me so you can get an idea of who I am and where I come from.

Born in 1989, I grew up with the country life in a little town in southwest Michigan, we were part of the "single stop-light" club. I was raised by my Grandparents, who adopted me at an early age and added their last name, Trapp, to my birth name.

I never felt privileged or entitled, we always had just enough and that's all we needed.

My Grandfather was a mechanic for a semi-truck leasing agency and my Grandmother worked in an applesauce factory. Your assumptions are correct, money was not pouring from the closets.

My Grandmother always taught me to save, save, save and that's exactly what I did. I understood the importance of having money, even at a young age, which is why I was mowing lawns and doing odd jobs whenever I could, just saving every penny. Before I was 10 years old I had my own bank account and by the age of 14 I had over $10,000 in savings.

I respected the value of a dollar and learned to scrutinize every purchase to make sure I wasn't just throwing my hard-earned money away. I also never talked about my money, to anyone.

It wasn't until late middle school to early high school when I realized that my understanding of money was above average. My friends were just now learning to drive for the first time, maybe opening a bank account and trying to save up for that first car. Meanwhile, I was entering trade school, to learn machining, so I could have a solid career out of high school. Right before graduation, I sat down one evening and made a choice.

The way I saw it, I had three options after high school: College, Work or the Military.

Everyone pushes college and to get that magic degree so you can be someone in this world. For me, college meant studying hard but working even harder to pay for it, since my Grandparents could never afford to. I didn't see the value in college.

Entering the workforce was promising, especially when I had a focused trade that would earn me more money at entry-level. I saw plenty of value in this but I also knew the economy in Michigan was not the best and I would ultimately end up just making enough, but not enough to really enjoy life.

Finally, the Military. I decided on the Military for a couple reasons… and no college was not one of them.

At the time of graduation, I was overweight and had low self-confidence, I wanted to change that. I also wanted to do something different from the same old "go to college, get a job, get married, buy a house" mentality.

The Infantry considerably changed my appearance, health and self-confidence. I was also deployed to Iraq in 2008, just 2 weeks fresh out of basic training. Obviously, my Grandparents were terrified but they supported me and my decisions.

I turned 19 in a combat zone when most of my friends were still figuring out how to fill out a financial assistance form for college. That year of my life seems like a distant dream, to this day, but I attribute a great deal of maturity and enlightenment to that one year in Iraq.

Once I returned to the States, I decided to move to Texas and start in the workforce. As of 2018, I'm still here in Dallas / Fort Worth, TX but the past 10 years will be covered in my next book.

Great! Now that we are well acquainted, let's get to why we're here.

Preface

I'm writing this book to address the concerning amount of ignorance and confusion around money and basic financial skills.

I know what you're thinking…

"Oh great, another get rich quick / investment how to book"

or maybe even

"Why do I need this book, I know how money works".

This book is not about getting rich or investing. Even if you think you know how money works, I encourage you to read on… there may still be something for you.

I have realized a serious need for financial education, even since I was young. Why is this?

Simple, money and finance are not taught in school or by many parents. It is an issue that has been debated many times and I'm not here to talk about why schools should or should not teach finances.

I'm here to teach you what your teachers and your momma didn't.

In the following chapters, I'll take you through a monetary journey of being financially uninformed to becoming the money know-it-all that will have all your friends and family asking you for advice.

Here is great place to mention that I am not a licensed CPA or Financial Consultant and I am not responsible for any financial decisions that are made using the teaching from this book.

Use logic and reason when making monetary decisions and if something doesn't feel right, it probably isn't.

Chapter 1
Money, the Glue That Binds Us

Money money everywhere but not a cent to spare.

This tends to be the rationale of most people in the world, however, money is very simple, either you have or you don't.

In today's society, having money is no different than having oxygen. I think most people would agree with that statement. Money determines how well you can live, where you can live, where you can go and how you get there. Money also plays a huge part in the rise and fall of countries and governments, alike. Even if we were to abolish money tomorrow, the world would still find something to barter back and forth as currency.

This means money is not a thing you have or don't have, money is an idea.

The idea of money is that the more you have the happier you are and that is partly true. However, without the necessary knowledge and skills to keep that money or be able to get more on a regular basis then happiness turns to depression and a bright life begins to dwindle.

I believe that money should be classified as an essential part of life such as air, food, water and shelter because quality of life and money are directly correlated.

Good news! Money is abundant! A bold statement, allow me to explain.

If I were to ask you for a $1000, right now… do you have it? And if so, would you just give me $1000?

I can't say whether you have a $1000 but I would bet you a $1000 that you wouldn't just cough it up to a stranger.

What if I were to ask 10 people for $100 each? This scenario seems more attainable but even $100 is a lot of money to just give to a stranger.

Let's take it a step further and ask 100 people for $10. Now we're making some money! It's still a stretch that the first 100 people you ask for $10 would give it to you but far more likely than $100 or $1000.

Final option… ask 1000 people for $1 each. Tried and true and the entire basis of every panhandler and pyramid scheme on earth.

Now, ask yourself how many people you know and of those people how many would give you a dollar. Almost everyone, right now, has the potential of nearly $1000 in a single day just because people and relationships are plentiful.

"Alone We Can Do So Little; Together We Can Do So Much."

–Helen Keller

Chapter 2

The Basics Everyone Should Know

This section will not turn you into an expert financial analyst or a certified public accountant (CPA).

The intention of this chapter is to elevate the financially uninformed or misinformed to a basic level of understanding and competency.

Imagine a world where everyone understood money…

----------SAVING----------

Stockpiling money in the bank, in a jar, in a safe, in a drawer or under your mattress is the most basic way to save money.

The hardest part is to forget that you have it when life's little temptations come whispering.

----------BANK ACCOUNTS----------

Opening a first bank account is one of the coolest feelings for a young person, it establishes a sense of responsibility and ownership.

If you don't have a bank account, go open one A.S.A.P.

Local banks are the easiest way to open a bank account. Just simply walk in to a few different banks in your hometown and ask to speak to someone about opening an account, they will walk you through the process. If you are just starting out, any bank should do, unless you already know of one you prefer.

If you plan to only save money, get a <u>savings account</u> which will yield a slightly higher interest return rate on the money you store there but will charge fees if you pull out money too often.

Plan on moving your money in and out a lot? Go with a <u>checking account.</u> These accounts usually do not have deposit/withdrawal limits but do not provide as much interest, if any, on the money stored.

----------BANK DEPOSITS----------

Cash - Bank Teller

Walk into your bank, fill out a deposit slip with the date, bank account number, amount to deposit and signature and take it to the Bank Teller. Make sure to have your ID with you.

Cash – ATM

If you don't have an ATM Debit card, you can skip this option.

At the ATM, insert your debit card and enter your pin. Choose deposit and insert cash in the designated slot. This option usually only allows up to 30 or so bills at a time. Make sure to count your money beforehand so you know what should be being deposited on the summary screen.

Check – Bank Teller

Slightly different than cash. You will still fill out the deposit slip with date, account number and amount to deposit with signature. Again, have your ID.

Now, you will need to "endorse" your check. This means you sign the back of the check in the space provided which essentially confirms that you are the intended person to receive the check and you are agreeing to the amount stated on the front.

Depending on which bank the check came from, the money could immediately "clear" or might need two to three days to "clear". This means the bank is verifying the check is real and the payer's account has the necessary funds to pay you. Check verifications can be problematic, since you will not have the funds available until the check clears.

Check – ATM

Similar to cash on the ATM, you will need to endorse the check then follow the instructions on the ATM to insert the check in the designated slot and confirm. There are cases where an ATM cannot read a check and you will need to use a Bank Teller instead.

Check – Mobile Phone

It is now possible to deposit money via mobile phone.

Depending on the bank you have, you might have this option available to you. Simply login to your bank's application or website and look for a mobile deposit option. This will activate the camera on your phone and you will take a picture of the front and back of the check, separately. You will still need to endorse your check and you may need to add your bank account number below your endorsement. Once pictures are complete, you will be asked for the amount of the check and to submit.

NOTE: You will need a contrasting background for the check and clear pictures, otherwise the deposit may not allow you to continue.

Direct Deposit

Direct deposit is the preferred payment method by most employers. A direct deposit is essentially a wire transfer of funds from the paying party to the recipient. No ID, No ATM, No Bank Tellers… Just cold hard digital cash!

To set up a direct deposit, your employer or whomever will most likely have a direct deposit form that you will need to fill out. For this, you will need your bank account number, routing number, bank name and whether you have a checking or savings account.

----------BANK WITHDRAWALS----------

Cash – Bank Teller

Visit your bank and fill out a withdrawal slip. This will include the date, account number, amount you want to withdrawal and a signature. Bring your ID and take everything to the Bank Teller.

Cash – ATM

If you don't have an ATM Debit card, you can skip this option.

At the ATM, insert your debit card and enter your pin. Choose withdrawal, specify whether you have a checking or savings account then enter the amount or select one of the provided quick draw options (usually in $20 increments).

If you are using an ATM that is not your bank's ATM, you will most likely have to pay a fee ($2 to $3) to withdrawal money.

Debit Card – Direct from Account

Purchases can be made directly with an ATM debit card. The money will be pulled directly from the linked account, this is the next best thing to cash.

Check – Direct from Account

Before you start yelling "Who even writes checks anymore!?"

YOU NEED TO KNOW HOW TO WRITE A PAPER CHECK!

Checks are still used every day, especially when buying homes or other large purchases.

You will need a checking account for checks and can just ask a Bank Teller, at your bank, to order you some. (there may be a small fee, but most of the time checks are free)

Let us begin:

1. Fill in the current date (or future date if you want to postdate the check)
2. Fill in the name of the business or person you are paying
3. Fill in the amount you are paying (using a dash or squiggly line after the cents so no one can add digits to your amount)
4. Write out the amount you are paying, this is a secondary verification of the amount so even if someone changes the numbered amount, it is much more difficult to alter a spelled-out amount.

   Examples:
   > Eight and 15/100 for $8.15
   > Eight Hundred and Fifty for $850.00
   > Eight Thousand One Hundred Fifty and 15/100 for $8,150.15

5. Signature – should match the name printed on the top left of the check.
6. Memo is optional, a brief explanation of the transaction

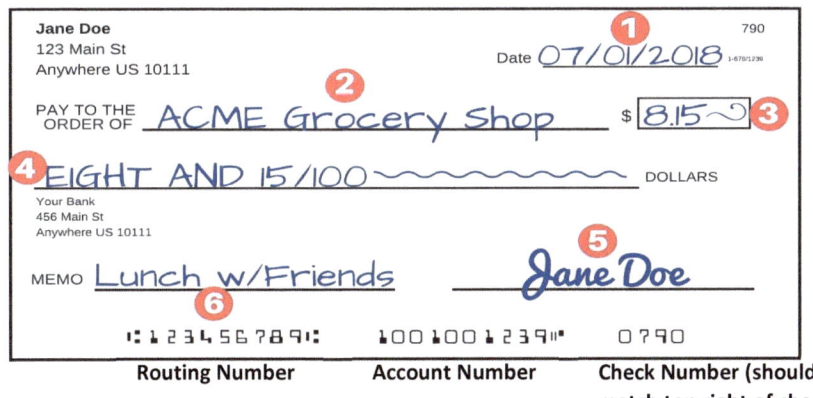

Direct Withdrawal

Direct withdrawals are preferred by most billing departments and credit companies. This is essentially a digital check, which transfers funds from your account to pay a bill or purchase online, using sites like PayPal. You will definitely want to set this up on a checking account and not a savings account.

For a direct withdrawal, you will most likely need to fill out a form that will include bank account number, routing number and bank name

What? You don't know your bank account number or routing number? Go look at the check image again, this information is at the bottom of every physical check.

Automatic payments are the best way to keep from missing payments.

----------CREDIT----------

What is Credit?

Credit is a financial score which reflects who you are in regard to financial responsibility.

FICO is the main credit score used and is calculated by looking at multiple variables including but not limited to: number of accounts, amount of open vs closed accounts, average length of time accounts are open before being closed, number of missed payments, number of defaults, etc.

Credit scores directly reflect the amount of financial risk a person conveys. The higher the score, the better the person's financial responsibility and vice-versa.

Why Do I Need Credit?

You might be the nicest person in the world but if you have bad credit it will be very difficult for you to move through life.

It is important to distinguish bad credit from no credit.

> No credit means you have no credit history, which can be built up and does not damage your financial profile.

> Bad credit means credit mistakes, which severely damages your credit profile and takes a long time to repair and recover.

Why Do I Need Credit? (Continued)

Credit is used anytime a financial risk needs to be assessed: Renting a house/apartment, buying a car, buying a home, buying a boat/motorcycle or any other large purchase that needs to be financed.

Even some employers check credit.

How Do I Get Credit?

Credit-Builder Loans, Personal Loans, Auto Loans, Credit Cards and Rent are some ways.

<u>Credit-Builder Loans</u> are offered by some banks and essentially place a sum of money in an account which repays the loan over time. Obviously, this isn't free, there will still be interest to pay over the lifetime of the loan.

<u>Personal Loans</u> might be hard to get with no or bad credit but basically lend you cash of which you can use for whatever you want. Saving the cash and repaying the loan would be very similar to a Credit-Builder Loan.

<u>Auto Loans</u> make up the majority of first ever loans for people. An auto loan can be obtained when buying your first car but will almost always require a co-signer since you probably have no credit.

<u>Low Limit Credit Cards</u> can be obtained ($200 to $500 limits) or you can get someone to add you as an authorized user on their existing credit card. The credit from that point on will be credited to both parties, so make sure they have good spending/paying habits. Age restrictions may apply.

<u>Rent</u> can contribute to a credit score. It is common for landlords to report rent to credit bureaus but you might want to ask when you go to look at a place, to see if they report or not.

The Importance of Credit

As mentioned before, credit is used during most of life's important purchases (house, car, etc.)

While it is possible to live with no or bad credit (a lot of people do), it will ultimately be much easier to take control of your financial profile and allow yourself the feeling of freedom whenever you need to submit a credit application.

How to Keep Credit

Easy! Make your payments on-time and in full. In the first couple of years of building credit, don't pay anything off early. You need to do the time to get the credit. Good credit doesn't just happen overnight... but bad credit can. Keep that in mind!

Keep credit applications to a minimum. Every time you submit a credit application, your score takes a small hit.

When using credit cards, it is important to never carry a balance more than 30% of the total credit line amount from month to month. The term "maxed-out" is used when stating a credit line has been used to its full potential. Holding a maxed-out balance tells the credit bureau that you are unable to pay down the balance from month to month, which says you are a risky client and therefore decreases your credit score.

----------CREDIT CARDS----------

What is a Credit Card?

A credit card is similar to your ATM debit card. However, a credit card is linked to a separate account that maintains a specified credit limit and is not cash. Once you spend up to the credit limit, you are out of "money" and will need to pay down the balance before you can buy anything else.

Again, holding a maxed-out card for more than a month is ill-advised.

Why Do I Need a Credit Card?

You Don't! No one ever needs a credit card. However, a credit card makes things easier when emergency purchases need to be made. (tire blowout, car repairs, medical emergencies, etc.)

You can also use credit cards to "finance" larger purchases that otherwise do not have a financing option, by purchasing with a credit card and then paying the amount off over several weeks or months.

How Do I Get a Credit Card?

Acquiring a credit card can be done at your local bank but there may be age restrictions. You can also apply for retail credit cards at most of your favorite retail stores.

Getting someone you know to add you to their credit account works as well and you can be issued a card with your name on it. Be careful, all purchases from either person will be charged on the same account. This is like sharing minutes on a cell phone plan, except minute overages don't hurt your credit score.

How Many Credit Cards Should I have?

There really is no limit but use common sense. It is always better to pay cash when cash is an option. All credit purchases incur interest, which means you will pay more for the item than if you would have paid with cash.

Credit is essentially spending money you don't have yet and you pay a price for it.

Why are Credit Cards Bad?

Credit Cards are not bad, they can be a very powerful tool in your financial arsenal. Just like most things, credit cards can be very dangerous in the wrong hands but, at this point, you should be informed well enough to use credit responsibly.

What is APR?

<u>Annual Percentage Rate</u> (APR), is used to calculate the amount interest you will need to pay on any purchases you make with a credit card or loan.

There are two different types of APR, Fixed Rate and Variable Rate.

> <u>Fixed rate APR</u> means the interest percentage is locked in and doesn't change.
>
> <u>Variable rate APR</u> means the interest percentage can change monthly, quarterly or annually in either direction. (usually increasing)

Always take a fixed rate APR over a variable rate APR whenever possible.

What is APR? (Continued)

A good rule of thumb for APR is anything below 10% is a good APR, 10% to 15% is a fair APR and anything above 15% is very high and you should avoid this kind of credit.

Essentially, the higher the APR, the longer it will take to pay off the balance, using minimum payments, because more of your payment goes toward interest instead of the original purchase amount. Higher APR can also greatly increase the minimum amount you have to pay every month.

----------LOANS----------

What is a Loan?

A <u>loan</u> is similar to a credit card. A loan allows you to borrow money that you don't have, to make a purchase.

Loans come in a couple forms, secured and unsecured.

> An <u>unsecured loan</u> is where a lender (bank or person) lends you money without collateral.

> A <u>secured loan</u> always has collateral.

<u>Collateral</u> is a physical object that the lender can take from you (repossess) if or when you do not pay back the loan. Usually the item being financed by the loan is the collateral. This could be your house, car, couch, etc.

Obviously, a secured loan is preferred by most, if not all, lenders. This makes unsecured loans a little harder to get. You will need a good/great FICO score and very clean credit history to borrow unsecured money.

How do I get a Loan?

You can visit any bank and ask to speak to a loan officer. Depending on the bank, they may require you to have an existing account with them and again, age restrictions may apply.

<u>Financing</u> any large purchase like a house, car, boat, etc. will result in a loan.

What is a Loan Term?

A <u>loan term</u> is the amount of time it will take you to pay back a loan, if you stick to the minimum payments. Loan terms are usually measured in months or years.

Normally, the longer the term the smaller the monthly payment. (Payment size is calculated using APR, loan term and total amount being borrowed)

If you are researching a large purchase, google "loan payment calculator" and you will be able to estimate what your monthly payment might be, based on APR, term and loan amount.

Loan terms are usually limited by amount being borrowed. The higher the borrowed amount, the longer you receive to pay it back and vice-versa.

Do Loans Have Interest Too?

Yes! Loans have interest too, and the same rules apply. Take fixed over variable APR and stay below 10% if you can.

Payments for both loans and credit cards consist of two factors: Principal and Interest.

> <u>Principal</u> is the original balance you borrowed (cost of purchase).
>
> <u>Interest</u> is the calculated price you pay for borrowing money (APR).

When a loan or credit card is paid, the interest is always paid first (profit for the lender) and then the remainder of your payment goes to the principal. This is why it takes so long to pay off borrowed money, you essentially take one step forward and two steps back with every payment.

The easiest way to offset this pattern is to pay an extra payment directly to the principal amount, every month, which will both lower the amount you owe and the amount of calculated interest you need to pay on the next payment.

Why Do I Need a Loan?

Again, you don't! Although, many purchases in your life will be done by financing, unless you have considerable amounts of cash and can just pay for things outright.

What is Refinancing?

Refinancing is the act of re-borrowing against an existing loan.

This is usually done for two reasons, lower monthly payments or transfer a loan balance to another lender.

After paying on a loan for about a year or if you have been paying extra payments, to pay down faster, then you might want to refinance your loan to drop your monthly payments. This works because the refinance loan will be for a lower amount than the original loan and will reset the loan term. Once you factor in the lower amount and longer remaining term, then the payment goes down.

----------DEBT----------

What is Debt?

Debt is the amount of money that you have borrowed and still owe. This applies to any form of credit card, credit line or loan you may have borrowed.

Why is Debt Bad?

Not all debt is bad.

> Bad debt is basically any purchase that does not retain equity.

> Good debt is any purchase that retains equity.

What is Equity?

Equity is the amount of value that an item retains, even after the borrowed money is paid back. Some examples of equity are houses (when bought not rented), cars, boats, some types of furniture, etc. When someone buys an object that retains equity it is called an investment because the buyer can at any point get money back out of that object by selling (also called "liquidating")

It is important to know that equity is not constant. This means that equity can either appreciate or depreciate over time.

What is Appreciation & Depreciation?

Appreciation is when the equity (value) of something increases over time. This is usually the case with land and houses.

Depreciation is when the equity (value) of something decreases over time. Nearly everything other than land and houses depreciates.

This is where smart investing comes into play because you should invest your money in things that will appreciate or things that will only depreciate a small amount.

A brand-new car depreciates nearly 20% from the original value in the first year of ownership and up to 60% from the original value in the first five years.

Consider the average auto loan has a term of 60 to 72 months (5 to 6 years). This means that by the time you have paid the car off, your car is maybe only worth 40% of the price you originally paid.

Example:

> Let's assume the average price of a new car in 2018 is $24,000.
>
> Using our depreciation stats from above, this means your new car will be worth $19,200 after the first year and only be worth $9,600 after 5 years.

Keep this in mind next time you are trying to decide between buying a new or used vehicle. The used vehicle has already depreciated, meaning you might get a much better deal.

How Do I Get Out of Debt?

Getting out of debt is a major industry. People sell books, courses, etc. all based around getting out of debt.

There are "tricks", I suppose, but the easiest way is to control the debt you acquire, in the beginning, and focus on paying debt down rapidly with extra payments.

Sticking to the minimum payment will help you build credit in the first couple of years but will prolong the time it takes to pay off a balance and ultimately costs you more in interest. This goes back to the one step forward two steps back principle we talked about earlier.

I realize there are plenty of complex ideas in the financial realm that I did not cover here but for the purposes of this book and my original intention of educating you on the basics of money, you should now be respectably informed.

Let's move on!

"When I was young, I had to learn the fundamentals of basketball. You can have all the physical ability in the world, but you still have to know the fundamentals"

—Michael Jordan

Chapter 3
The "B" Word

Let us welcome the Queen B of finances… Budgeting!

I know, I know… no one likes to be told that they should budget, or diet, or moderate their life in any way, shape or form.

If you do not budget, you will go broke, end up with bad credit and just maybe… have to move back in with your parents.

Now, as much as your parents love you and you love them, no one wants to have to do the walk of shame back to their parents and say, "I failed".

I would say this an extreme case but, unfortunately, it happens every day.

Budgeting is not a scary Queen B... budgeting is very simple and consists of two factors: Income and Expenses.

<u>Income</u> is any cash flow that you currently receive, whether it's on a regular basis or not.

> A few examples of income are: paychecks, allowance and cash for services such as mowing lawns or odd jobs.

<u>Expenses</u> are anything that require you to spend money. Be careful, not all expenses are obvious.

> Some examples of expenses are: phone bill, car payment, insurance payment, rent or mortgage, water & electricity.

Pretty easy, huh?! What about these less obvious expenses...

> Gas for your car (anytime you leave your house, you spend money by using gas)
>
> Food/groceries (most humans eat multiple times a day, all that is expense)
>
> Animal food (do you have pets? They gotta eat too and that costs money)
>
> Fun (do you golf, go to the movies, park downtown... all cost money).

As you can see, life can be expensive... funny how expense is built right into the word expensive.

If you don't have a clear grasp of all your income and expenses then you are probably not budgeting as well as you could and you might be heading for rough seas in the near future. (better start remembering mom's birthday!)

Let me walk you through a very easy way to assess your current financial situation and determine whether your budget is need of an overhaul.

The Income:

First write down how much money you get every month (after taxes). I usually only count the regularly based income that way I don't rely on spontaneous income for regularly based expenses.

The Expenses:

If you use cash daily, this will be hard, but not impossible. If you use some kind of electronic payment, then you should be able to export all your expenses for the past year or several months from your bank.

Begin sorting out all the expenses you have every month, either what you can think of or the things you see pop up on the bank statement every month and write them down (name/description and amount).

Once you have this list, sit back, take a breath and realize how much you actually spend every month… this may be shocking for some.

The Math:

To assess your current financial situation, you need to subtract total monthly expenses from the total monthly income. Hopefully the resulting number is positive.

> If the result is positive, you are said to be in the "green". This means you have a positive cash flow every month and you are in good shape, but could maybe do better.

> If the result is negative, you are said to be in the "red". This means you have a negative cash flow and definitely need to change something.

Now, if you are in the red every month, the only reason you aren't broke yet is because you had initial savings that are slowing being chiseled away by the negative balance every month. This is what causes the majority of Americans to be living paycheck to paycheck.

Before we get into how to fix your budget, let me talk a little about "living within your means".

This phrase is considered derogatory by most and is offensive simply because people feel you are telling them how to live their life.

I completely agree with "living within your means". If you don't, you end up in the red every month and have to move back in with your parents.

It may not happen today, this year or in the next 5 years… but negative cash flow will destroy your finances, eventually.

Example:

The first car is an **Economy Class Sedan** that costs $18,599.00 and the second car is a **Luxury Sports** car that costs $49,999.00. Let's assume the financing option available to you is a very good **6% Fixed APR** for **72 Months** with $0 money down.

Take a moment to google an auto loan calculator and plug those numbers in to see what the monthly payment will be…

You should have gotten the following:

Car 1: $308.00 per Month / Car 2: $829.00 per Month

Now if you make enough income every month to spend an additional $520 on a luxury sports car and still be in the green… then, by all means, go for it! However, realize that a luxury sports car cost more to insure every month and needs the most expensive gas, which means after the not so obvious expenses, you may break even or be in the red.

This is what it means to "live within your means", simply do not spend more than you can afford or continuously sustain. Now, does this mean never use credit cards or take loans?

No, but do so wisely and with calculated reason.

Now, back to fixing that budget! (or starting one...)

You already know your monthly income and expenses, you should have them listed out with names/descriptions and amounts.

Income is a little more difficult to modify since it entails getting a raise, better paying job or doing extra work, like a second job.

If you have an opportunity to do any of these, then do so.

Split your expenses into two categories: Debt and Revolving.

<u>Debt</u> should include anything that you could pay off, if you won the lottery tomorrow.

<u>Revolving</u> should include all the ongoing bills that can't be paid off: food, electricity, water, phone, insurance, etc.

Once you have the two expense categories separated, sort each category by monthly amount (most to least).

Now that you have a clear picture of your monthly expenses, begin brainstorming ways to decrease your revolving expenses.

Some possibilities might be:

Switch phone service providers or request a phone bill decrease. (phone companies can and will lower your bill, but not if you never ask)

Switch electric companies. (look for first time customer deals that have drastically lower rates)

Re-evaluate your insurance policy. (increasing deductibles can lower your insurance premiums but be careful, in the event of an accident you will need to pay more out of pocket)

Examine your fun activities (movies, golf, etc.) and determine whether you can moderate a little.

The idea is to get creative and research ways on how to lower those monthly expenses that everyone has.

Next, begin brainstorming ways to decrease your debt expenses.

> Whether you can refinance to lower the monthly payment or grab a second job for additional income to pay off debt, either is a great strategy.

> Here's another great idea! Take that annual tax refund and dump it on your debt!

> Pay off as much as you can in one shot or at least payoff the debt that costs you most every month (debt with highest monthly payment). This will equate to instant monthly savings, almost like getting a raise without having to sweet talk the boss!

Remember!... none of this will work if you do not take action. Once you have your ideas brainstormed, go out and fix that budget!

"Do you know how many athletes go broke three years after they stop playing? I want to help them hold on to their money. I mean, I know about budgets."

—Jay-Z

Final Thoughts from Me to You

Throughout the journey of this book, you have gone from financially uninformed to be able to take on the world.

Again, I'm not a certified expert… but I do see a need for monetary education, especially within my generation.

I feel like the world believes that if you don't know something then you should go educate yourself. I partially agree with that idea but there are some of us out there that don't realize we need help until we're almost out of reach, financially. (broke, in debt and terrible credit profiles)

Whether you're a Millennial, Centennial or Gen-X… I hope that you enjoyed the contents of this book and that you gained some enlightenment from it.

I encourage you to take your new-found knowledge and bestow it upon everyone you know or at least those that you feel need it… and please spread word of this book and what it's taught you.

Imagine a world where everyone understood money…

Oh… and keep an eye out for my next book, a look at how I increased my income by $20,000 a year, every year, for the last 4 years.

"Knowledge, like air, is vital to life. Like air, no one should be denied it."
—Alan Moore

www.ingramcontent.com/pod-product-compliance
Lightning Source LLC
Chambersburg PA
CBHW040259220526
45473CB00002B/533